# Signs, Translations
# John Hildebidle

**salmon**poetry

Published in 2008 by
Salmon Poetry,
Cliffs of Moher, County Clare, Ireland
Website: www.salmonpoetry.com
Email: info@salmonpoetry.com

Copyright © John Hildebidle, 2008

ISBN 978-1-903392-83-6

All rights reserved. No part of this publication may be reproduced or transmitted in any form or by any means, electronic or mechanical, including photography, recording, or any information storage or retrieval system, without permission in writing from the publisher. The book is sold subject to the condition that it shall not, by way of trade or otherwise, be lent, resold or otherwise circulated without the publisher's prior consent in any form of binding or cover other than that in which it is published and without a similar condition, including this condition, being imposed on the subsequent purchaser.

Cover photography: John Hildebidle
Cover design & typesetting: Siobhán Hutson

*Look! The world is so numerous.*
COLBY BROWN

*All around us are signs; some even have translations.*
ED BARRETT

*[T]o pay attention is to behold the wonder*
A. R. AMMONS

*Niki, Nick, Susannah:*
*all and everything*

# Acknowledgments

Thanks are due to the editors of the following volumes and journals, in which poems from this collection first appeared:

*Defined Providence, Witness and Wait, Dan River Anthology*, and *The Old Chore*.

Particular thanks are due to my friend and colleague Peter Child, who included "Snow Buddha" in his song cycle "Bleak Light".

The sustaining friendship of Every Other Thursday helped shape many of these poems—when I ignored that advice, it was always to my loss.

A special thank you to the crew in Knockeven—Jessie, Siobhán, Tim, the dogs, and most particularly the inestimable Eve.

The Dean of MIT's School of Humanities, Arts, and Social Sciences kindly provided financial support for the final stages of the production of this book.

# Contents

*Starting Points*

| | |
|---|---|
| All New | 15 |
| Arrival | 16 |

*i. just these sights and sounds*

| | |
|---|---|
| Along the Path | 21 |
| Beach Glass | 22 |
| Bird Paranoia | 23 |
| Blizzard Games | 24 |
| Knowledge Foresworn | 26 |
| Mocker | 27 |
| Dove Song | 28 |
| Rehearsal | 29 |
| Possum at Twilight | 30 |
| The Feast of the Verification of the Crocus | 31 |
| Particular Effects of Morning Light | 32 |
| Unexpectedly | 33 |
| I Recognized Him as a Neighbour | 34 |
| "Like Rome, This Town..." | 35 |
| Rooflines | 36 |
| Slinky Homework | 37 |
| Windows | 38 |
| Just Exactly As It Happened | 39 |
| T. L. McGuire, Decorative Painter | 40 |

## ii. as and where I live

| | |
|---|---|
| Transition | 43 |
| Sitting on Sunday Morning, Sipping Coffee | 44 |
| Her Dressing-Table, Like An Old-Style Altar | 45 |
| Across | 46 |
| Fads, Styles, Fashions | 47 |
| The Girl at the Mirror | 48 |
| "Let the Good Times Roll" | 49 |
| "How Could Anybody **Live** Like That?" | 50 |
| Two Paintings by Charles Sheeler | 51 |
| Johnny Mudge | 52 |
| Family Legend | 53 |
| In Passing | 54 |
| In Front of St. John the Evangelist's | 56 |
| Habañera | 57 |
| Poet and Infant, Once | 58 |
| A Vocation, Same As Priest or Lawyer | 59 |

## iii. a good traveller

| | |
|---|---|
| *Bus Turistic* | 63 |
| Adventurers | 64 |
| Speciality of the House | 65 |
| The Youngest | 66 |
| The Town Parade | 67 |
| Family Weekend | 68 |
| Effects of Wind and Sun | 69 |
| *Degustibus Rapidus* | 70 |
| The Sunny Southwest | 71 |

*iv. repossession:*
*poems on the life of Henry David Thoreau*

| | |
|---|---|
| April | 75 |
| July and After | 77 |
| November | 79 |
| December | 80 |
| Mid-Year | 81 |
| May | 83 |
| Marker | 84 |

*v. postcards*

| | |
|---|---|
| Accumulation | 87 |
| The Binary System | 88 |
| Living in Detail | 90 |
| Hesitation | 91 |

# Starting Points

## All New

*"Here comes the sun ..."* After a long
prom-night: white limos, corsage,
handsome date, first white dress shirt,
tie with an authentic Italian label.

Forget this hill was once the dump.
Now, filled, landscaped, it's a mock-drumlin,
just here at the ice-age-edge. First light,
in near-summer, the green almost hurts,

it's so absolute. Almost the end
of the beginning: watching fresh colours,
a girl on each arm, at ease, no edge of competition.
Possibilities. *"... and it's all right."*

*For Nick*

# Arrival

As a child, like you I moved—
never so vastly, of course,
but again and again and
until it became something
deeper than habit.

Even nowadays, all grown,
once a year at least
I move all the furniture,
a mock-repossession.
With practice I grew

adept at arrival's work,
reading landscapes
of gesture, custom, sound,
until they became an inner
and sensible language

that let me, always moving,
come to a sort of rest.
But never, till now, was I
the thing come to.
As I sit, this evening,

while in the next room
the bed creaks as dreams take you,
and the sun climbs so affably
branch by branch down trees
full of homebody jays

it feels like the time
for confirmings of title.
while I sort out what you might need
(nothing too weak, too common;
just enough for an overnight bag)

to recall what you saw, a few months back:
the tall guy with glasses,
counting out the first steps of welcome,
baffled under the stare of his new,
surest claimant.

*for Susannah, on her second birthday, and first with us*

## ii. just these sights and sounds

*Why should just these sights & sounds accompany our life?*
Thoreau's journal, April 18, 1852

# Along the Path

> *So quickly, without a moment's warning,*
> *does the miraculous swerve and point to us.*
>     MARY OLIVER

Why only that one wall, just the one section?
Don't paints fade? Surely that wild lavender
can't date back to when this was
a sleepy rail right-of-way, and nobody cared
if kids spent half the day wall-painting.
Now, does somebody (armed with ladders and pails)
come by moonlight, silently, to awaken
that auroral blending, those coded hieroglyphs?

I'm almost moved to take up jogging, to pass by
more often, dawn or nightfall, to wonder.
That handbill—"This path will close
March 24-31 to allow demolition
of an adjacent building"—pray it's an April Fool's Joke.

# Beach Glass

Unlucky? Inattentive? Not patient enough?
However, whyever it happens, I never find any.
But perseverance? I have it to burn.

Scallop shells (nickel a ton)? Certainly.
Dead kelp, the odd Wellington,
rocks that shine like gems until they dry.
At least it's off-season, so poptops
and Bud cans are rare, blessedly.
And the memories aren't missing:  honeymoon
beach-walks, tiddly on Zinfandel;  an infant son
bent on devouring the whole beach;  risking
the actual, chilly Sound water in relief
from reading *War and Peace*;  sunsets.
And, yes, a daughter's ashes,
put into the wind by the rock just up ahead.

Maybe the point is *not* to have a point.
You'd think altruism would count for something—
I think it's ugly, but she dotes on it;
I'm chasing love tokens, you could say.

*for Niki*

# Bird Paranoia

I suppose they have to, small as they are.
But maybe it's delighted curiosity
that keeps them watching us, night after night,
through the smallest lighted crack between drapes.
I can't kick the sheets aside, on a hot night,
without thinking some pervert bluejay is gawking.
And that pigeon who favours the windowsill
what exactly does he have in mind?
*Voyeur* sparrows, peeping finches, crows
(surreptitiously quiet) come closer, closer,
well within focus length.  I suppose
there's no need to worry, though
how can they spill the beans? But what if
(what when) some damned scientist learns
at long last to decipher bird song?
Isn't that a knowing smirk
in the eye of the swooping he-cardinal?
And how like snooping reporters
those jays seem, once I look at them more closely.

# Blizzard Games

Let's dream it summer,
        make of the wind a warm, soft glove
                with nothing better to do

than fondle a cheek or thigh.
        The grimy ice-piles we can melt off
                just by keeping our eyes above street-level,

pretending the sky's sharp winter-blue
        is high, cloudless August.
                Let's be blind to the season,

deaf to the weather; joyfully
        ignoring the world and its moods,
                even the crackle of news-broadcasts.

Let's lean back, half-dressed
        into summer's lethargy
                as if we were floating

on some currentless pond.
        Think of the sun, butter-yellow,
                dappling our arms, the trees

chortling with birds,
        the windows open wide to catch
                every slightest breeze,

so the grumble of traffic
        and now and then the gripe
                of some neighbour dog

fills the room. The sheet's too much,
    weighs on our feet. Month after month
        we'll dream of cold

so the dreams curl back on themselves:
    winter to summer to winter,
        a perfect closed loop of comfort.

So what if the windows rattle
    in a breeze. To hell with wind-chills.
        To hell with ice-patches on every walk.

We'll make summer wherever,
    whenever, however we can, and smile
        at its worst days, knowing their worth.

# Knowledge Foresworn

I read it somewhere—birds don't sleep long hours,
so "waking at dawn" is only the way we wilfully
misread the noise. They've learned how night-silence
fools predators. Come light, they can rely
on camouflage and air-speed; and sing.

Still, it's a healing falsehood: each morning the world
awakens, as we do, and possibility is reborn, unscuffed—
the sort of legend we need. So, this morning,
well short of five A. M., two hours before the thunder,
 the world woke, and with it every singing bird.

# Mocker

Four years searching. Nothing but soured hopes.
I'd heard him, often enough,
grandly sporting from song to song.
But by the look of it, you'd think
this is strictly jay country,
whole trees full, allowing only the odd sparrow.
I'd just about given up, really,

Then, last Tuesday, off as always to the subway,
I passed the corner street-sign, hardly
worth a glance. But there, ample and bold,
as if asserting principality,
he sat, peered down at me,
flicked an indifferent tail, flew,
all with a grey-brown benevolence.

# Dove Song

Too soon, too soon, too soon—across
the rising hiss of street traffic
that demands a new day.
Mournful? Hardly, least of all
in the vaguely-light of early morning.
Someone must have misheard morning.
No bereavement, purest seduction:
*Isn't there time, just barely time,*
*before the alarm insists?*
*Why not, why not, why not?*

# Rehearsal

*for Polly*

There had been talk about fixing up the barn—
but nobody had a clue who actually owned it,
or its true age, or history. Just a barn,
ample, faded, derelict. Skunks were fond of it,
swallows as well. The squirrels had grown bored.
Some muttered about rats.

It was hotter than anyone could remember.
Then, near dawn, out of nowhere, came the smell of
    a fireplace.
Bells, bustle—the barn was in flames. "Fully involved"
(we soon learned the lingo). We were sure at first
Kenny Burcheski had been sneaking a smoke
and ditched the butt carelessly, but, no, the fellow
in the grand uniform explained it was a careful torch-job,
so the volunteers could hone their dousery. Drew a crowd.
The hiss of steam almost hurt your ears,
heat could raise a blister from across the street.
It finally collapsed with a sigh and a crash all at once.
From then on, just mop-up.

We'd drunk all the lemonade, eaten
the ham-and-half-sour sandwiches.
The Good Humour man had stopped cruising by.
Still, a successful, even triumphant day,
except for the swallows. Our one chance
to see the gauze of cataclysm, that close.
Next morning, we prowled the ashes,
collecting melted nails. And one shape
Kenny kept insisting had been a horseshoe.

# Possum at Twilight

This is hardly wilderness—barely a block one way,
the hum of the main drag, and even nearer runs
    commuter-rail.
Still, we've no lack of nature—skunks, mockingbirds,
raccoons the size of small bears, that regal pair
of nesting cardinals, crooning mourning doves,
coal-black squirrels, litigious as any of their kind,
and one more, pure white but black-eyed, so no albino.

Now this fellow, balancing his way down the fence-top,
rat-nosed and rat-tailed, the colour of a dusty ghost,
enduring totem of the clan of Imperturbable Atavism.

# The Feast of the Verification of the Crocus

Snow-drops in slush? How apt.
But crocus, especially
the regal purple,
buried in snow, or caught
in a twilight decaying
into mock-November? Pure
eco-sarcasm, no premonition,
a scar of delay.

Until

the light unslants itself,
clouds relent, vibrant spikes
(yellow, white, that grand striped
item, with a thimble of melted
butter inside) stand
attested, even gloating.

Surely
this is the day
we've all
earned!

# Particular Effects of Morning Light

Haze molds the streetscape,
leaving the familiar strangely
unrecognizable.
Brick never seemed so kind.
Neon, now, smiles affably.

Out on the turnpike, fog
descends, thick, unforgiving,
extreme. Eyes emerge
in place of taillights—the road
is a place of prowling beasts.

Then—gone. Clear sky, sun
on the rock of road-cuts, dyed
green, gold, grey: sandstone?
something with copper? Granite?
Why do we let the light so toy with the world?

# Unexpectedly

At first glance, I was sure it was stuffed,
or one of those plastic "keep the squirrels out of your
    strawberries"
owls you can pick up cheap at Home Depot. Perched on
    a fire-escape,
at the end of a dormitory hallway—hardly *Mutual of Omaha's
Wild Kingdom*, where one imagines such creatures ruling.
Then it moved, slowly, grandly, just its head, surveying
what it clearly took to be its own well-merited kingdom.
Peasants—well, all right, students and researchers,
stopped in their tracks *en route* to some dreary lab—
could only peer in amazement and ignorance. A red-tail,
surely—they favour this urban terrain.
Not so much a rare bird as a bird rarely, magnificently placed.
Proof, if it were needed, that *what is* will jolt you, every time.

We met twice more—once with him in grand flight,
larger, more elegant than ever a crow or gull,
once only by sound.
Ever the scholar, I sought advice:
"A courting Red-Tail," the expert said. "In transit."
So many blank walls (that's what appeals to him)
kept his call echoing, racking the nerves
of the local sparrow-and-finch population,
who could imagine becoming a snack,
so hopped from branch to branch to ground,
never risking a long flight or relaxation,
endlessly chirping the warning.
At the beach, once, I watched a flock of tiny,
impertinent terns worry off
an osprey no smaller than this.
But here, now, an insufficiency of heroes.

# I Recognized Him As A Neighbour

Usually, the signal is considerable perturbation—
sparrow, squirrel, cats mutter anxiously.
Today it was oddly quiet. He took his ease
on a low branch, then swooped down
nearly to pavement level. *A gull?* I thought,
at first. But no, not white enough. Pigeon?
Far too large. Rising, he spread his tail—
THAT'S where the name comes from!
A red-tail surveying his estates, then
set off into the trees behind a nearby house.
This time even the brazen crows sounded an alarm.

# "Like Rome, This Town

*for Marci Davis*

nestles among seven hills." This one's Allegory.
Mid-slope is the contemplative block:
chaste, faint yellow, cool aqua,
a pink which, if it were a rose,
you'd have to call "Virgin's Blush."
Down there, at the bottom,
the Slough of Pretense—*faux* stone,
paper brick, fibreglass guised as purest clapboard.
By the church on the summit, assertion rules.
Crayola blue, red, even purple encourage
the trim to shout. Each house shares
sharp peaks, inevitable,
foursquare porches, dented air conditioners,
meagre single chimneys (furnace,
not hearth). Now and then a geranium
or even a doorway asserts the personal,
alongside a continuing indifference of traffic.

# Rooflines

*for Vicki Kocher Paret*

All down this comfortable, a little seedy street,
the castellated houses lounge at their ease.
How can such amplitude, such near-pride,
not annoy? And yet the certainty calms.

*Gambrel*—somehow like the thigh of a horse
or the hook you'd use to hang a side of beef.
So bloody, so rustic, for a genteel New England roof!
*Hipped*—not wide bottomed—but angled, a thing
of two slopes, as if at odds with itself. *Mansard*
after its proud French deviser, but sanded down
into American speech. Wrapped in a hidden
flashing, secure. *Gable, pitch, eave*—
the words make their exact steps, sure to the knowing,
lost to those of us walking to work,
idly glancing up in a chilly spring sun.

How firmly they rest, the words, like a stack
of four-bys, waiting—*quoin, portico,*
*architrave, pediment*. Each just
shaped to its work. *Dentate,*
like the teeth of a guardian dragon.
Perhaps, for style, *a porte cochere,*
or, higher, *Palladian* window, Renaissance
among cedar shingles. At the top, *ridge pole,*
*summer beam, dormer* make sleep easy. "This is the house ..."
and none just precisely its like, each
girded with sure timbers of speech.

# Slinky Homework

Who could know?
    Who wanted to calculate—
        an interfering carpet, a riser
            three quarters of an inch too steep,
                Try and try and try and try, failure
                      always followed.
              Pray it's no paradigm.
          Again. Assignment. Any dolt
      can accomplish. No talent demanded,
    perfect! Halfway, further, **momentum**!!
Stall. Cease. Halt.
    Again. What luck refuses, talent resists,
        stubbornness will gain.
            Surely.
                Abandon hope. *Try, try again* grows
                  foolhardy. Toss it aside,
                      Turn elsewhere. Wait!
                          One step, two, three,
                  half a dozen. All the way,
              top to bottom!
            The key revealed:
        purest inattention. What you don't want
    happens readily.

# Windows

*from the hilltop highrise*

crescent moon, just rising, bright
as a slit in a blackout screen. What
were eaves and yards and parks
darken to mock-stars. Sunset
plays out the cloud pretense
that endings are bold, grand.

*street level*

I'm no peeper, mind you, but you can't
keep from looking through bright, uncurtained
windows, at overpainted mantels, candles
in chianti bottles, pantries (door ajar)
full of half-eaten cereal boxes:

I know the place, even at this distance—
know the book open on the crate table,
the pizza halfeaten next to the phone
the shape looming just out of sight:
myself. It is, for certain, each
scruffy apartment I ever lived in. The view
out from inside is pity and indifference.

*home*

It's all wrong-end-to: inside, full dark,
outside oddly light, scratching at the windows,
the pale steady glow of an insomniac moon,
helped by yellowed streetlights. A box
of smudged sky, mysterious noisy trees,
a yard too well-lit by a forgotten lantern,
and when the clouds blow away, that one planet,
too bright to be a star, too still to be a plane,
toying with the waning moon, like a kid
with a yo-yo working *round the world*.

# Just Exactly How It Happened

*for Nan, from "Baby Brother"*

As ever the college wiseass, I didn't even try
not to read it as dark, comical omen,
when my sister fainted during her wedding.
Discreetly, kneeling at the altar, just a slump
to one side. The hearty priest signaled the altar-boy
—was this a customary event?—who scurried back
with a tumbler of water. *Excitement*, was the party line.
*Denial*, I imagined. *Cowardice, even. Feet so cold
you could shatter them.* I was projecting, of course.

The marriage did go sour, but the life didn't—
three fine sons, another wedding,
a knack as a grandmother. I have a new theory
—am I projecting, still?—pure, giddy optimism.

# T. L. McGuire, Decorative Painter

As though by some Rule of Contrast—he *was* his house.
Tiny and thin, not tall and angular,
still he suited the place, and the other way round.
It was identical to all the houses—
"row houses" then, no doubt "town houses" now—
on the block; but he was an anomaly,
the only Irishman in a family of Dutchman,
the one New Englander surrounded by,
drowning in Philadelphians.
He went his own way, and the house—*inside*—
did too. The Stromberg-Carlson took up
half the parlour. The windows were closed tight
all summer, shades drawn, "to keep
the heat out." Air too.

He held court in the kitchen,
sipping a quart of Schlitz. Aunt Addie
firmly disapproved, forbade him
to walk to the corner to buy it,
harangued us when we brought along
a bottle wrapped in brown paper.

He carved, painted ("Pennsylvania
Dutch Hex Signs a Specialty" his sign said),
repaired his pipes with Plastic Wood,
which always unsettled me.
Taught me, they say, to walk,
by tying a string to my belt and waiting.
His house was him because he was it,
and himself, and satisfactory both ways.

# ii. as and where I live

*Out of what one sees and hears and out*
*Of what one feels, who could have thought to make*
*So many selves, so many sensuous worlds,*
*As if the air, the mid-day air, was swarming*
*With the metaphysical changes that occur,*
*Merely in living as and where we live.*
    Wallace Stevens

# Transition

*to Niki*

But I, if anyone, should have it down
cold by now, like Dad packing to travel:
how many moves? How many plans?
Who's counting? The in-betweenity,
the absence of sure place jars yet.
All packed, books, doodads,
the picture of my Irish grandfather
in his oval frame, the flat Scituate rock,
the mason jar of carved corks—
laid up in courses
like granite for a pyramid.

Why can't I lay my hands on things,
recover the reassuring order
of accidents of a life, to get through
the spin of matters hour by hour?
How long is the wait?

When we find ourselves again,
we'll argue about whether
to hang the pictures straight off,
or hesitate, think it through,
see how the light falls;
carp about why we threw *that*
(of all things) away,
*It would fit so perfectly
in that corner, no longer
to be stumbled over.*
And something will disappear
*Which box? Which damned box?*
until we've all but given up hope.

I can hear you insisting *It'll turn up.*
True, perhaps, but infuriating for all that.
"I want everything, and I want it *now!*"

# Sitting on Sunday Morning, Sipping Coffee

Fooled by a sun that whispers "May," in March,
the chill off this concrete sidewalk bench must
be hard on her, the bundled woman just there,
hunched next to a stuffed plastic bag.
The poor can be so *visible*.
Passers keep eyes on shopwindows—
squash-rackets, bouquets, art books.
I could say hello or give *something*.
But when at last I stroll by,
on her far, hard-to-see side stands
a proper suitcase, not even scuffed.
I've misread her: she's just idling,
 before she catches the train
to see a few New York shows
or spoil grandkids in Niantic.
I'd better move, or miss the sermon.
Does she kill time inventing me a life?

# Her Dressing-Table,
# Like An Old-Style Altar

A thing of such glass and perfume.
Three mirrors make many of her,

while she brushes out, even in summer heat,
that hair—floor-length! A smile toys
with her mouth. Does she know I'm a spy at the door?

She always lets me do what I want,
while we make our yearly visit.
My mother grumbles. Poppop, worn

but genial, slips me quarters
to take to the corner for snow-cones
and chats with George, who rocks

and tells stories of when Babe Ruth
was a schoolboy wonder. Two years ago
George gave me a mitt the shape of no other

I've seen, the smell of leather long-used
and accommodating. Even in the morning,
dead still and already hot, I was second up

—just after her—to creep down
the carpeted hall and watch,

in devotion and puzzlement. So many bottles,
each stoppered with glass. Once I snuck in
at midday and opened every last one,

and let dizziness roll over me like a fine cooling wind.
"Such work, such work, Little One. To stay beautiful,"
as the brush slid electrically down and again down.

# Across

*for JML*

"It's no accident, that garden—the wall of the yard,
tall as a man, curves precisely behind it,
and the sidewalk edge is trimmed, straight, tended.
The garden itself could, at first, be a patch
of unusually healthy weeds—but then you notice
tomatoes, runner beans, zucchini, decorative blossoms.
From the upstairs window where I've put my desk,
it's a parable.But we preachers lean to such thoughts
Sometimes a mother pauses a stroller
for vegetable lessons.  Students pass in numbers,
rarely glancing, full of rich self-involvement,
on occasion fingering a leaf, as if suspecting plastic.
Once, only, a short fellow in overalls
reached out and plucked a tomato (surely the best)
and strode off, unabashed, unpunished.,
and (as he imagined) wholly unobserved."

# Fads, Styles, Fashions

Bell-bottoms, tie-dyed tees—they were
easy to junk. My mother still dusts with them,
gets an odd dreamy look, starts singing,
"Monday, Monday." She calls it singing.

The rhinestone in my navel was more like it—
especially with that fishnet halter-top: an eye-catcher,
for sure. Drove my dad right up the wall, but my brother's
college roommate suddenly thought I was a star.

Still, once it was gone, the hole healed up. No
commitment, really. But **this**—I can just imagine
when I've been stuck in some Rest Home, they'll
all stare, and ask for a decoding (the wierdo

who did it gave me a half-hour epic, about sun signs
and the Cabala, but who has time for that? A snake with wings,
seven stars, a sort of cloud—make up your own story,
    if you want.)
My always-sensible sister wonders, "What if you change
    your mind,

or decide to wear a satin, off-the-shoulder sheath, to some
    ritzy spot?
What then?" Regrets? Why waste time. I can look down,
at my very own arm, and wear pride like mascara:
*Once, at least, I had guts.* There's the proof, plain as day.

# The Girl at the Mirror

*for Susan*

So gentle and small a painting—I'm almost ashamed to look.
Her clothes are something soft like linen; they hang
at her waist while she sits at the dressing table
seeing to that wonderful long ample hair.
Her breasts must be small, almost invisible,
if her back weren't turned, if the mirror
didn't reach barely as low as her chin.
She hoards her privacy, and justly so.
But those open windows—isn't there
some young fellow—the scamp!—
who's shinnied up a tree for a glimpse?

Her back has the arc of promise.  I can without trouble
imagine a mole beneath her rib cage, a fine down on her belly.
Is that a smile of remembrance? If I had any manners,
I'd look away, turn back to the actual world.
But I cannot, and to tell the truth, don't want to.
She's dreaming, it's easy to see that.  So
why can't I, for the moment, do the same?

# "Let The Good Times Roll"

Rhythm? Hardly a trace of it.
Bad dye job on her hair, dress
not so much dirty as just shy of clean,
a woman "of years" dances,
—snaking her arms, rolling her hips,
prances—or a rhumba?—across the plaza.
Two guitarists, young, lean, and talented,
lay down a good sound.
They want nothing to do with the dancer,
she's just making use of them.
Nobody else stops to look.
Nobody stops to laugh: who's
she bothering, anyhow?
A stately black woman, coming up
 from the Subway station, mutters,
"That's mojo, and she's got it working for certain."

# "How Could Anybody **Live** Like That?"

Here, anything you could sell is long gone. This world
    is pure chassis,
burnished by smoke, wind, a little acid rain. I rigged up
    the tarp
maybe fifteen years ago. She asked me to. Trained the
    two rats
(Verne and Margo) when the cat ran off. I mean, you
    get lonely.

The cops like me, though—I scare off the crackheads
and guys looking to drop off a corpse. They call me
    "Fido," and laugh.
Let them. I've been called worse, and by better.
Food? Steal? I call it *recycling*. And at least some crip or wino

gets my share at the soup kitchen. Charity, in a way.
Selflessness. Sister Betty might even be proud
of her influence. The library card I found, I admit—but
    it works.
I'm halfway through Wodehouse, at the moment.

Conrad, Lardner, a little Trollope, all that Dickens.
One thing I have lots of is time, after all.
Miss her? Of course, but then again no. She's not here,
    I know—
I don't hallucinate. But I can remember
every last sweet inch and twitch of her,

any time I want, day or night. No, it's not a bad life.
Low overhead, you might say. You play the hand they deal
    you, right?
Hey—somebody just ditched that Camry,
and torched it. A regular light show.
Just about every damned night. Who needs video?
    I've got live.

# Two Painters by Charles Sheeler

*"New England Irrelevancies"*

All geometry, all light. Brick, necessarily.
The feasibility of a ladder. But no sign
of rock, foliage, chickadee, gull.
Is it what's here or what's not that's
beside (outside) the point?
The label mutters about abandoned mills,
economics. The surety of edges
mounts into bafflements.


*"View of New York"*

So much of a window, foursquare and open,
almost melting into the outside air.
The canvas chair is sturdy but not welcoming.
That hooded shape on the right—an abandoned camera,
we're advised—could be sewing-machine, printing press,
mangle. The ceiling light is abrupt, unadorned.
A studio? No sign of spattered paint or drafts
hung for reconsideration on any wall.
So much light, so much uncertainty,
tied to a sole brown perpendicularity.

# Johnny Mudge

*for Nan*

He could make things work I didn't even
know had names.  When winter moonlight made city
roofs shiver, he'd be at the Sunoco,
sure, waiting, like some angel-messenger.

One night my sister said she'd fallen for him.
Silence owned the dinner table.  She'd been
the one who planned on teaching.  This was
her Elvis moment.  But when blond, high-cheeked Alan

strolled by, it was, "Goodnight, Johnny."
—until she was sitting on the sofa, waiting
for her prom date (after ten. Even I'd
figured out the truth) and who was it who rang
the doorbell? At the curb, somebody's Chevy,
tuned to perfection, red as promises.

# Family Legend

Great-Uncle Montell, Baltimore Irish to the heart,
had no legs. When his oil truck ran afoul of a trolley,
quick cutting was the only way to get him out
ahead of the explosion. Propped on a stool,
he tended bar at the family Speak. A master
of homebrew. Every so often,
some blowhard would start to bitch about the tab,
look down, and say the unforgivable: "If you
weren't half a man, I'd ..." Montell could, so they say,
swing himself up onto the bar top with one hand,
reach down for a sawn-off baseball bat with the other,
and calmly say, "Have you met my equalizer?"

# In Passing

It's not (I'm sure of it) that he's small and Asian,
nor even anxious, that makes him seem ancient
beyond any calculus I know. He's dressed for the weather—

the air's chilly, but the sun's bright—in one of those
red-and-black check woodsman's wool jackets,
and one button resists him. He *is* ancient,

or near enough, and his anxiety's not small, for sure.
The air's chill, even in the bright sun, reason enough
to fight that button, even if his fingers long

for the grace of a zipper. With the face
of no Maine guide ever born, he could be dressed
precisely for the weather, if only that damned button

or those small fingers would do their duty. Should I offer
to help? How, without seeming rude? What code
of smiles and gestures could leap across age

and continents, past anxious embarrassment, to ease
this nagging dilemma? I don't know him—he's
not the old fellow I often pass playing lethargic

tennis with a woman I presume is his wife
nor yet the "he" of the couple up the block,
who sit proudly on their stoop beaming toward

what must be two fine grandsons, on bikes or roller blades.
A stranger, and ancient, so small and anxious, his outfit,
weather-perfect, coming up just short, against chilly air.

All I can offer is a sort of quiet prayer, "Safe home,"
where a doting grand-daughter can brew him some hot tea
and plump the pillows on his favourite chair, while he tells her

of his adventure on the Avenue, with that troublesome button,
the chilly air whistling into his opened jacket, the sun bright
but not warm, and the large passing stranger who stared.

# In Front of St. John the Evangelist's

His hair pale and delicate, he bends over
a walking stick, looks somehow *familiar*, yet not.
I debate rousing conversation, wonder how.

'Hello' would have to do. His speech gives him away:
"You're not from around here." "Then again,
you're not either." We form an easy union
of estrangement, sealed by his trove of preacher jokes.

"I was a missionary. Ill health put a stop to it."
He's swum counter to the tide, migrating north.
"Not that bad, except for the first winter, two years ago.
They'd warned me the motto up here is, 'Live, Freeze,
and Die.' Can't convince them that's just New Hampshire."
By now we're firm friends. "Had a spring in your step,
this morning, Preacher." "Off to MacDonald's, for coffee.
They always and only talk about the weather, there.
Never quite happy, come rain or shine.

Kind of makes you glad you're not God, doesn't it?"

# Habañera

*after a family dinner at "the home"*

"This lady used to be an *opera* singer!"
"Indeed I was. (Distractedly, she pats her clothes—
lost keys? a list, a scribbled memo crumpled in a pocket?)
Have you seen her? My daughter. I know she's here."
(we make noncommittal noises. Her clothes match, only just,
as if she had to keep them firmly in mind or they'd fly
into disparate paisleys. She smiles) "Are you *Polish*?
That boy (my son) has the map of Poland on his face."
(We wait for her to wander off. She heads out into the dark
cold night. Shouldn't someone help her? Worry
deepens her slouch. None of our affair. A relief
when she comes back, though).
In time, from the "Friendship parlour,"
a piano, firmly played, but slowly. Familiar—dah dah
dah **DUM**. dah dah dah **DUM**. dah dah dah dadayada
**DUMDUMDUM**. Oh, yes—Bizet! At last, her voice—
the marks of long training, but drifting aside
from true mezzo. "*L'amour,* **L'amour.**
Cadenza. Pause for recognition. Two passers-by ("neighbours,"
they call them here), in loud voices only the old
and the very young can afford, insist, "Well, at least,
she's **better**. A little." "Next, Sir Arthur Sullivan."

# Poet and Infant, Once

*a photograph in a biography of Robert Lowell*

Head to head, on an unannouncing carpet,
the two of them, an unlikely match.
He's forty, his hair coal-dark and curly,
a dashing profile, though his face is shadowed.
Her head has the round, bald promise of infancy,
full of the accomplishment of upright looking,
eyes wide, in full and eager possession.
For the moment, they're just on the level.

It's a common scene: father and daughter.
But where's the self-laceration that made him?
She perhaps has this framed, on a wall,
seeing only the pride on his face,
as though that erased the dark years,
as though fathering were healable, now.

# A Vocation, Same as Priest or Lawyer

*for Tom Lynch and Charlie Keefe*

"Change my name? No way.
You play the hand that's dealt.
Billy's dad was in the trade,
so learning was easy to arrange.
Ah. The secrets you can learn,
the reputations you can wiggle,
with powder and a fresh shirt.
And the thrill of your name
on a sign on a wide-front house:
*O'Brien, Wilson, and Fudge: Funerals*

# iii. a good traveller

*A good traveler has no fixed plans and is not intent upon arriving.*
    Lao Tzu

## Bus Turistic

*Much welcome to our excellent city*
(we circle a vastly mythological fountain,
honouring the hero of some indecisive battle.
It seems that here not to lose is to win).
*The chronicles say he died bravely. The legends*
*promise he will return at the hour of our greatest need.*
(That's a sweet, understated church,
Romanesque the guidebook says,
dedicated to "the patroness of futile altruisms.")
*In this square, in August, all the people gather to pray*
*for the relievings of an overcast day.*
*The musics are quite distinctive...*
*No one can say who first lived here.*
*The sea breezes. The wonderful port,*
*rivers leading far inland,*
*rich soil—always this has been a place*
*of human gathering* (and perspiration).
*We will wonderfully greet you*
*when you come back, as you will.*
*To find so much changed,*
*all—this is a certainty—for the better.*
*During the meanwhile, be having a fine day.*

# The Adventurers

*for David*

A narrow street (but then they're all narrow) in the "Old City."
That unsettling too-bright late evening when Spaniards dine.
An amble to see what we'd encounter off the worn path.

They stepped out firmly, arm in arm, lean, crisply-dressed,
serenely past seventy. Serious but not dour. Exploring, too.
But those white canes—the admonition *no tocar* must
    chafe especially;

They call on no guide, consult no Brailled map. Confident, eager,
open to discovery, they offer a rebuke to my sorrowful lethargies.
They need no directions (do they even speak the languages?).

They fall back, calmly, on their own resources.
And besides, if you come down to it, they have each other.

# Speciality of the House

It looked like nothing I'd ever eaten.
Surely that word on the menu meant pork.
The waiter tried so hard to explain.
My wife smirked, visibly:
"How is it? (No innocent question.)"
"*What* is it, I'd like to know."
"He told you. Pig's feet. Didn't you understand?"
We sipped some wine.
"You mean you knew that I was doing
and let me go right ahead?"
"You're a big boy." "And often a bigger dolt,
as you know well. I rely on you to rescue me."
"A full-time job, and more besides."
"All that was called for in this case was a subtle hint."
"Was it that bad?" "I won't say, one way or another.
That's your punishment." "You ate it all, and it was
'the Specialty of the House.' Consider it an adventure."

# The Youngest

*Near Bruree, County Limerick*

Stephen and Elizabeth, prospering at University,
were tourist-brochure perfect, the two of them:
well-knit, handsome, athletic, eager to do their share
in the barn and kitchen. Then there was Jimmy,

just somehow "off," his body twisted, his speech
hard to decipher. He didn't go in much for reading.
But he could drive the herd to the barn, fork
out silage, and when he sat high

on the Massey-Ferguson, driving down
the long drive between the hedgerows,
he had the family smile, every inch of it.

His father, hosing the milking-stalls,
offered an introduction to the visiting Yankee:
"That's my lad Jimmy. Such a worker.
We have big hopes for him."

# The Town Parade

in South Bristol, Maine, is late.
An old guy—hawk-featured, his trousers worn
and dark with the work of lobstering—

paces the route, on the lookout for something.
Once, twice past, then back the opposite way.
Have the volunteer firemen and the schoolboy band
gotten lost? At least the weather makes it
a good day for idle chat.

Behind me a group tells yarns decked with names
—Poole, Paradis, Sproul—that have a native tang.
"You remember the guy, years ago, who used to
walk backwards around Lewiston? Hour after hour,
always talking silently to whomever.
You could have a good conversation with him—
not addled or drunk or anything.
But never explained. A sort of local landmark."

A tour guide for ghosts? I see him now,
clean-shaven but a bit too bright in the eye,
his hands working the edge of his pockets.
Not a stumble, not a nod, high tide or neap.
Maybe nobody had the gall to ask him.

# Family Weekend

A dark road
despite the moon.
Overhangs of trees
slice roadside signs

into a set for a cheap thriller.
We cursed ourselves
for skipping a dry run
in full daylight.
Around a blind curve,

a dark line across the asphalt.
Branch? Shadow?
No, my wife, driver-naturalist,
decides, "Snake."
Alive? Dead? Sluggish

in autumn night-chill?
Indifferent to mortality and traffic?
We had a destination,
no time for nature-study.
We'd see if it had moved,

on our way home. But that
was hours later, darker.
Had it been *there*, where
some colonist left behind
an historical marker?

Or *there*, where sewer pipes
awaited the improvers' efforts?
No sign that we could see.
Maybe he'd hitched a ride.
Or turned back into pure omen.

# Effects of Wind and Sun

The last few leaves, outside the windows,
twirl madly—they can't hold on much longer
against the thrum on the house, hearty
and insistent, that makes the sky play instability

variations: cloud, rain, light. Stippling whitecaps
buffet skiffs that rest like paperweights
on dirty paper, tugging their painters.
Safely inside, a book, a mug of cocoa

offer sufficiency. Tonight the cross-cove lights
will dance, and maybe, just maybe
it will clear enough so the moon, nearly full,
can grandly occupy its prideful, deserved place.

*Bailey's Island, Maine*

## *Degustibus Rapidus*

Too soon, too late, too stubborn,
the coyote fails every single time.
Even the elements conspire: lightning
*will* strike the candy cane dynamite
A joy in sheer plotting, but the glitch
glitches: mistimed diesel, rock
falling six inches off, the chain of devices
astounds, then misfires. A parable?
Of persistence rebuked,
but proof against any thwart?
Of futility self-renewing, perdurable?
Such a pointless effort—but then
from across the street,
whose goal wouldn't seem
enigmatic, even comical?

# The Sunny Southwest

Fiesta—The biggest of local deals. The town square, usually owned by pigeons and drunks, wears balloons, ribbons, booths. Ray-bans are very big, and for once nobody fears rubbing shoulders—emigré retirees, *Mexicanos*, 'Indians' (Well-schooled, I flinched at the label. But my guide said, "I don't care what you call me, as long as you stop crapping all over me"). *Enchiladas, tortillas, quesadillas, fajitas*: sweet taste-music, with lots of *jalapeños*. On the corner, the busiest booth of them all—selling, it grandly announces on a hand-written sign, "The World's Best Kielbasa Burritos." Who'd be presumptuous enough to argue?

# iv. repossession

poems on the life of Henry David Thoreau

*"Nature is a haunted house—but Art—
a house that tries to be haunted."*
    Emily Dickinson

# April

Burning (had the wind stayed true) the town,
the one home he hated well
enough never to leave, he'd grown
careless with matches, like some swell

city-stale, who on a rotty
stump cooked chowder in a spring drought—
the grass flared in an instant chest high
and where the pines lined out

the pasture, the fire bloomed orange
like a demon autumn. He found
it just the thing after eating
his fill of fish and bird-song

and once it was well-caught
he had two things to do (he
loved the pure paradoxicality
of taking both sides at once).

He ran in the alarm
and lay back to watch, always
the joyous eye, as the prim farms
went like tinder, and his companion prayed

it wouldn't burn Town Meeting. Henry figured
you could find worse things to sear.
He could see he'd by luck cornered
a name that would wear

and one rich in angles as a fallen barn:
"Tree-burner Thoreau," of all
things, or as it settled out, "damned rascal"
for sooting the town's linen—

well, he could piece out the steps
for doing that job to a turn,
breeding a practice Apocalypse,
and in very good place and season.

# July and after

Sage Emerson was over
viewing the old world, and hired
Alcott to build him a summer
house. Alcott soared

on inspiration and designed,
to honour the Muses, a nine-
cornered cottage,
and to hell with the straightedge.

Henry worked double to cure
the meanderings of that capacious
mind; Alcott dreamed as ever
but had to get his hands, alas,

*in* the thing, while Henry put in more
shoulder and less brain—
moral building, each nail sure
at one stroke. Fresh from his own

house-work, just man-shaped
and left at the pond for loons,
he worked all summer. For the town
it beat a horse-pull: boys skipped

fishing to watch the thinkers
clamber on the skewed ridge-
pole like squirrels summer-
drunk. Even Henry laughed,

"Ah, he's a crooked stick." Let
Alcott hear if he deigned to—
Henry knew crooked and
from the inside.  In time

the Great Man smiled on the house,
and ignored it.  Birds found it
risky but still useful
for nesting, and it stood

years, weed-grown, curious,
a landmark of sorts, too
damp to burn, sagging to compost,
held, as Henry guessed,

true to form by his nails
and serene geometry.

# November

Calling in autumn on *that*
*Walt Whitman, of the scribbling gentry,*
who at first was not home, Henry
went to the kitchen and, flat-

out, asked Walt's mother for hotcakes.
Whitman, great contradiction-darer,
fretted until he died about that lapse
in bourgeois manners.

When they did meet, words came hard.
Henry, all nose, found
the poet broad but not fine.
Whitman, who hoarded

a nation's body in his own,
down to the teeth and sweat,
guessed the fellow from Concord
knew man only in abstraction.

Imagine their talk: the Universal
Raver, dressed like a woodman
even in sidewalked Brooklyn;
older, stubby of body and soul,

Henry in stiff city-cloth,
who'd rather have numbered Walt's hairs
or laid a notched stick across
that beefy hand to take its measure:

"I feel, I feel, the voices great within me!"
"Aye, but know ye muskrats?"

# December

*I discover a strange track in the snow.*
Enough snow to cover, not to hinder.
A familiar yard, in town, near the smithy.

Not so strange after all—creature with few, quiet myths,
not lion, not eagle, not grizzly. Just otter.
Cousin to his beloved muskrat.

His delight astounds even him, perhaps.
No simplifying, this once. *Each instant*
*is full of great events,*
even in the fallen world of Concord.

Can such extravagance withstand the cold December air?
To the prepared, the out-landish eye, indeed.
*I am thus reminded*
*that every chink and cranny of nature*
*is full to overflowing.*

# Mid-year

Dead summer, and the air sags from use.
His tramps persist. Heavy with dust,
as if the earth rose to claim
anything fool enough to roam,

he collects what little promise
the near shore can offer.
Apples are weeks off, and harvest;
farther still, the winter rigor.

There is now only the past
of seed to be lived out.
For miles roundabout
walking moves from one waste

to the next. Weeds brittle in sun.
Cicadas moan over a few sour
early berries, not even worth
the picking. None

of the landscape quickens. What use
to keep at it? Why not lie down,
lazy as snakes, and risk sleeping
through this season of small fruits?

Then, today, after twenty years or so,
he learns a name, of the rush he'd seen
over and over but found no
one else could recognize, even

the reliable codgers. He'd
wondered if it were some by-
blow, a bastard shoot that only
he ever saw or pulled

to press in his sample-book,
a plant of the inner eye. But
no, and by accident, this finer
knowledge is his, making the shore

dance of a sudden to a communicable
step, while he scribbles,
full of the sap of that naming
which is the sole repossession.

# May

Declining in a canework cot, his own-
made, he is beyond naturalizing farmers' land.
Now he has the memory only
of short legs that could hurry

everyone else's down to stumps. Still,
he seems happy. No one understands,
with his future brief and all
indoors, shrunk to a parlor of maiden-

ladies and bric-a-brac, and the rabbit
pelt a boy brought last night,
thinking it might make him feel like
tramping again. He does it

and tells no one how;
collects—the rascal!—his and
our own dying, with so
much pleasure they'll hang

lessons on it he'd have sniffed
away in his good days. But now
with a great smile his beard
keeps under wraps, he has a last go

at making facts in-
to virtues, virtues into nails:
*"It's better. Some things should end."*

# Marker

Longing for places he wasn't wanted
he found enough nearby to keep
outrage well-stoked. He hunted
what no one could stomach: muskrat,

Irishman, himself; and what wouldn't be
drawn he wrote down, not afraid
of the common because even the least weed
would scratch someone. Ordinary,

and he knew it: one of the odd-
job men any town has, idlers
but handy, and proud of both;
proud too of the particular nowhere

he railed against; bathed
in antagonism as if in mossy
water; changed his name (but
only a little); travelled (but only

a little); made pencils and charts
and enemies and birch wine no one
else would drink and books that
mildewed in his attic, and

if no one listened still he shouted,
like a rook before sunup: **wake,
wake, wake, wake**—words
sure enough to split the husk.


NOTE: The poems on Thoreau derive from moments in his voluminous Journal. Direct quotations are indicated by italics.

## v. Postcards

*for Niki, always*

*Allow me to love
all of you.
It could take years.*
    Kim Vaeth

*at the very core of love — for another, from another — resides a necessary secret still point, an emptiness almost, a blank space not to be filled, a tale left untold.*
    Jonathan Strong

*I hope to stand with those who love
their lives in time to live them,
bravely, between kisses, under stars.*
    Robin Becker

# Accumulation

May-
be it's
what we're best
at: buying a-
nother book for the
awkward stack we plan to
read some summer, or a junk
shop table exactly right for
the cottage we'll never own, or one
more carved frog to catch dust on the plant shelf.
Snug in a midden of bargain life-
fill, safe from frost, fire, or slip up,
we catalog, imagine
whatever's from now on
junked or stolen, it's
certain to be
not love, not
soon, not
us.

# The Binary System

### 1.

When the colours first come up with the sun,
dark spring green still sits on the fiddleheads.
The marsh grass pretends to be a meadow,
and the white oak in the side yard, half dead,
manages new suckers to throw shadow
on its striplings. Each green variation
is weighted with the blue of deep water.

Of course there must be an August later,
when colours sour with heat and the air is
thick enough to fold. But this morning, this
green deserves not to be much thought over,
not to have future thrown like weed killer
on unexpected growth, but to be instead
left whole in a brief kindness of the sun.

*(June 1978)*

*2.*

Back, after adventure and some grief,
a month earlier than our habitual summers.
As ever, your naturalist's eye makes note
of views through what we always were
used to as thick woods.  More flower,
promise of heavy berrying.  Even I can hear
familiar birds—catbird, gull, towhee.

There's a rumour coyotes are only
a narrow Sound away.  Signs warn us—
**No Trespassing.  Posted.  Keep off the dunes.**
We manage to find the once-hidden,
nature trail we'd enjoyed with an infant,
now labelled, poshed up with parking.
A cairn on the beach reminds too clearly
of where we left a daughter's ashes.

It dawns, as we pack - we still
fit so well, here and together.
The relief is not all kindness is brief.

*(May 1998)*

# Living in Detail

In the drowsy moment just before morning
croaks itself awake with radio news,
you still dream that there is in everything

an order of grunts and jay calls.  Waking
you fight against, as if you could still choose
drowsing for hours, lifetimes, not just mornings

and in the warm blanket hollow you'd cling
congenially to that someone whose
snore and flank are just then quite everything

that answers the bulletins' muttering
now! into your ear, past her arm's loose
grip, drowsy, momentary, each morning

of this well-married defense in holding
hard to what needs no hot off the wire news
for that drowsy minute just before morning
which measures an order, an everything.

# Hesitation

Maybe just
the one quick
kiss. But
she's asleep. What if
I wake her,
not some spell-haunted princess,
but the overtired heart of the household?

Anxiety
grapples affection.
Why did I
stay awake so long
reading that half-baked novel, anyhow?
Missed opportunity.
Will a gentle
caress of a shoulder
serve?
*(Must.)*